A GIFT FOR:

Happy Birthday

FROM:

Ken + Judy

FRESH-CUT
Flowers
FOR
MOTHER

www.jcountryman.com
A division of Thomas Nelson, Inc.
www.thomasnelson.com

Copyright © 2002 by J. Countryman,
a division of Thomas Nelson, Inc., Nashville, Tennessee 37214

Compiled and edited by Terri Gibbs.

Designed by Garborg Design Works, Minneapolis, Minnesota

Photos by Lisa Garborg

www.thomasnelson.com

ISBN: 0-8499-9599-X

Printed and bound in USA.

Hundreds of dewdrops to greet the dawn,
Hundreds of bees in the purple clover,
Hundreds of butterflies on the lawn,
But only one mother the wide world over.

GEORGE COOPER

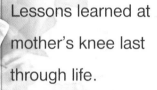

Lessons learned at
mother's knee last
through life.

LAURA INGALLS
WILDER

*Well, at least the ones you remember.
But it's funny how they keep popping
up now and then. Just when you need
them the most.*

*Where else can you go to find
comfort, acceptance, forgiveness,
encouragement, praise, and
consolation . . . all in one hug?*

Mother is the name for
God in the lips and
hearts of children.

WILLIAM THACKERAY

You respect me enough to be truthful, even when it is painful and unpleasant. I don't usually say so, but I appreciate it.

Mom is a tough friend. I know she is going to be honest with me.

ROBERT ELDRIDGE

The mother is and must be, whether she knows it or not, the greatest, strongest, and most lasting teacher her children have.

HANNAH WHITALL SMITH

Thanks for standing true to your own ideas and convictions. It has helped me be true to mine.

Love is, above all,

the gift of oneself.

JEAN ANOUILH

God gives us friends—
and that means much;
but far above all others,
the greatest of His gifts
to earth was when He
thought of mothers.

ANONYMOUS

*It is a gift that lasts
through all our days.*

One mother achieves more
than a hundred teachers.

YIDDISH PROVERB

Actually, I think
you achieved more
in my life than any
single teacher
I ever had.

*How comforting to think of the love
that always fills a mother's heart
and spills over into the home.*

Love begins at home.

MOTHER TERESA

Mother shone
for me like the
evening star—I
loved her dearly.

WINSTON
CHURCHILL

For me, you shine like an
entire star-filled sky glowing
with a golden moon.

Who ran to help me when I fell,

And would some pretty story tell,

Or kiss the place to make it well?

My Mother.

Her children rise up

and call her blessed.

PROVERBS 31:8

Who can ever measure
the benefit of a
mother's inspiration?

CHARLES R. SWINDOLL

*I owe heaven an
unpayable debt for giving
me a God-fearing mother.*

There is no friendship, no love, like that of the parent for the child.

HENRY WARD BEECHER

More than my mother,
you are my friend.
That makes me glad!

At times I remember, and reflect on my childhood. It amazes me and humbles me. I understand things better now.

How dear to this heart are the scenes of my childhood, when fond recollection presents them to view.

SAMUEL WOODWORTH

Mother's apron gave you
assurance. Rushing in
from school or play, even
if you didn't see or hear
her, you felt better just
finding that apron hanging
behind the kitchen door or
dangling across a chair.
Her apron, smelling of
cookies and starch and
Mother. It comforted you.
It made you feel secure.
It was part of her—like her
laugh or her eyes.

MARJORIE HOLMES

My mother's love for
me was so great
that I have worked
hard to justify it.

MARC CHAGALL

No matter how old we get, it is still
important to make mom proud.

You were never a perfect mother. I never had to be a perfect kid. Yet the love was always there, each for the other. What a relief to live in reality.

Children find comfort in flaws, ignorance, insecurities similar to their own. I love my mother for letting me see hers.

ERMA BOMBECK

Some are kissing mothers and some are scolding mothers, but it is love just the same, and most mothers kiss and scold together.

PEARL S. BUCK

And how wise the mother who does "scold and kiss together."

Nobody knows of the work it makes
To keep the home together,
Nobody knows of the steps it takes,
Nobody knows—but mother.

ANONYMOUS

You have to love your

children unselfishly.

That's hard.

But it's the only way.

BARBARA BUSH

I've known some selfish mothers,

which makes me realize how blessed

I am that mine is not!

A mother is like a veil: she
hides the faults of her children.

YIDDISH PROVERB

Where would I be today,
if not for your ability to look
beyond my faults and visualize
all my pent-up potential?

How great to have a mother
who is not only wise but clever!

An ounce of wisdom is worth

more than tons of cleverness.

BALTASAR GRACIAN

*I don't know how mothers
accomplish all they do.
They probably don't either!*

The word *mother* is
a synonym for some
of the hardest, most
demanding work
ever shouldered
by any human.

LIZ SMITH

A mother understands
what a child does not say.

ANONYMOUS

Even now you seem
to read my thoughts
and feel what my
heart feels, but cannot say.

*Time and again I find myself
wondering, "What would mother
do in this situation?"*

What we have learned

from others becomes our

own by reflection.

RALPH WALDO EMERSON

You taught me how
to live and learn from
the lives of others.

We are wise by

other people's

experience.

SAMUEL
RICHARDSON

Knowledge from books;

wisdom from life.

JEWISH PROVERB

We watch and want to be

the good that we see.

Now thank we all our God,

With hearts, and hands and voices,

Who wondrous things has done,

In whom His world rejoices;

Who from our mother's arms

Has blessed us on our way

With countless gifts of love,

And still is ours today.

MARTIN RINKART

The measure
of love is
compassion;
the measure
of compassion
is kindness.

ANONYMOUS

*I'm so touched by your
compassion, which reaches far
beyond our family to so many
who need a touch of kindness.*

Nothing means as
much as my dear
mother's tender touch.

Mothers must model
the tenderness we
need. Our world can't
find it anywhere else.

CHARLES R. SWINDOLL

Rain or shine, mother of mine, your love was always there when I needed it most.

A noble heart is a changeless heart.

ANONYMOUS

The memory of a well-spent
life never dies.

CICERO

I cannot keep you forever,
but the memories I can hold
close in my heart.

No woman can be strong,
gentle, pure, and good without
the world being better for it,
without somebody being
helped and comforted
by the very existence
of that goodness.

PHILLIPS BROOKS

*I could fill books with the
names of people who know you
care—and care deeply.*

You taught me to expect the most and believe the best. That gives me courage to face an uncertain future.

Whatever
enlarges
hope will
exalt
courage.

SAMUEL
JOHNSON

That habit of giving only
enhances the desire to give.

WALT WHITMAN

Your generous heart gives out
to others and makes them
want to give back to you.

They're only truly great
who are truly good.

GEORGE CHAPMAN

I think you're great,
because you're a truly
good mom!

The supreme
happiness of life is
the conviction that
we are loved; loved
for ourselves—
rather, loved in
spite of ourselves.

VICTOR HUGO

*Who can love us freckles,
phobias, and such . . . but our
blessedly biased mothers?*

In the final analysis it is
not what you do for your
children but what you
have taught them to do
for themselves that will
make them successful
human beings.

ANN LANDERS

I've always been glad that you
were never afraid to push me
out of the nest—and that you
waited until I could fly!

*I have no doubt God chuckled
to think of your surprising
personality, and sighed with
contentment to know what a
wonderful mother you'd be.*

When God thought of
Mother, He must have
laughed with satisfaction—
so rich, so deep, so full of
power and beauty was the
conception.

HENRY WARD BEECHER

Mothers are

quintessential people.

ALEXANDRA
STODDARD

Youth fades,
love droops,
the leaves of
friendship fall . . .
a mother's love
outlives them all.

OLIVER WENDELL
HOLMES

*Thank you for teaching
me that God is love, that
His love is never-ending.*

I remember my mother, my
father and the rest of us praying
together each evening. It is
God's greatest gift to the family.

MOTHER TERESA

Mama was like a flowing
river, blessing the banks
of life around her.

MARGARET JENSEN

Oh, God, for others let me be,
at least half the blessing
my dear Mother has been to me.

You filled my life
with the wealth of
wisdom that comes
from loving God.

No one is poor who
had a godly mother.

ABRAHAM LINCOLN

I certainly don't have to apologize for being one of your most ardent admirers.

A hero is someone we can admire without apology.

KITTY KELLEY

We are in truth,
more than
half what
we are by
imitation. The
great point is,
to choose good
models and to study
them with care.

LORD CHESTERFIELD

Mom, I choose you!

Joy is knowing your
mom loves you,
even (especially)
when you don't
deserve to be loved.

Blessed are

the joy-makers.

NATHANIEL
PARKER WILLIS

Hope, like the gleaming taper's light;

adorns and cheers our way.

and still, as darker grows the night,

emits a brighter ray.

OLIVER GOLDSMITH

Your kindness to me
let me see
how to be kind to others.

We are made

kind by

being kind.

ERIC HOFFER

How is it you always seem
to know exactly when I
need a glimmer of laughter
to chase away the gloom?

A good laugh

is sunshine in

a house.

WILLIAM
THACKERAY

We learn
only from
those whom
we love.

GOETHE

I'm still learning . . . still loving . . .
so grateful to be loved by you.

The child praises the mother.

The house
praises the
carpenter.

RALPH
WALDO
EMERSON

To serve is
beautiful, but
only if it is
done with joy
and a whole
heart and a
free mind.

PEARL S. BUCK

I can't count the times you
have served others, not
only joyfully but willingly.

When a woman puts her finger for the first time into the tiny hand of her baby and feels that helpless clutch that tightens her very heartstrings, she is born again with the newborn child.

KATE DOUGLAS WIGGIN

No one has given more to my
life than you, Mother.

Mother's love grows by giving.

CHARLES LAMB

Everything
I learned
about love,
I learned
from my
mother.

MARITA
GOLDEN

I learned things like
a hug can let you
know you're special.

You made our home a sanctuary—a haven from the hectic, harried, world outside.

The woman
is the heart
of the home.

MOTHER TERESA

There is no greater place
of ministry, position,
or power than that
of a mother.

PHIL WHISENHUNT

God could
use a few
more mothers,
like mine.

The wise woman builds her house.

PROVERBS 14:1

*The older I get, the more
I marvel at the work and
determination you poured into
making our house a home, not only
a beautiful home but a godly home.*

There is no more influential or powerful role on earth than a mother's.

CHARLES R. SWINDOLL

You have been one of the most positive and significant influences in my life. Thank you for being a wonderful role model.

I honor you mother. Not just for giving me life, but for making my life a gift.

Honor your father and mother, even as you honor God, for all three were partners in your creation.

JEWISH PROVERB

The shepherd always tries to persuade
the sheep that their interests and his
are the same.

STENDHAL

*A mom does the same thing
with her kids. Only she has
to be more subtle about it.*

To love someone more
dearly every day,
To help a wandering child
to find his way,
To ponder o'er a noble
thought and pray,
And smile when evening
falls—this is my task.

MAUDE LOUISE RAY

I always seek the good that is in people and leave the bad to Him who made mankind and knows how to round off the corners.

GOETHE'S MOTHER

How glad we can
be that God does
indeed let us leave
the rounding
off to Him.

She who gives all,

though but little,

gives much.

QUARLES

*Even when we didn't have much,
you taught us to give generously.
You were teaching us how to open
the door of God's rich blessings not
only for our lives but for others.*

Mom, you are truly
one of God's greatest
gifts to me.

I thank God for
my mother as for
no other gift of
His bestowing.

WILLARD

How beautiful
a day can be
when kindness
touches it!

ELLISTON

Mothers
have big
aprons—to
cover the
faults of their
children.

JEWISH
PROVERB

*Every kid needs a mother's
forgiving heart to hide behind.*

To be good is noble,
but to show others how
to be good is nobler.

MARK TWAIN

When I didn't listen to the good you said, I couldn't ignore the good you did.

I remember my mother's prayers . . . and they have clung to me all my life.

ABRAHAM LINCOLN

I will always count on your prayers, Mom.

If you were blessed with a
good mother, you will reap
the benefits all of your days.

CHARLES R. SWINDOLL

Mom, the legacy of your love
goes on and on and on.